Cryptid UK
(Monsters, Myths & Mysterious Beasts)

Prologue

In the quiet corners of the United Kingdom, where the shadows grow long and the mists hang heavy, there exist tales that defy explanation. Stories passed down through generations, whispered around campfires or shared in hushed tones over a pint in your cosy, local pub. These are tales of cryptids, monsters, myths, and legends - creatures that dwell just beyond the veil of our understanding.

Introduction

Welcome to a journey into the unknown. This book is an exploration of the strange and unexplained creature sightings that have occurred across the UK. From the depths of Loch Ness to the peaks of Ben MacDhui, from the quiet lanes of Norfolk to the rugged cliffs of Orkney, we delve into stories that have intrigued, terrified, and fascinated us for centuries.

Each chapter is dedicated to a unique creature or legend. We begin with perhaps the most famous cryptid of them all - the Loch Ness Monster - before venturing into lesser-known but equally captivating tales like the Owlman of Mawnan and the Lincolnshire Lizard.

This book is more than a mere collection of tales; it's a passport to the uncharted territories of the United Kingdom, where the line between reality and folklore blurs. It's an exploration of the enigmatic, the inexplicable, and the downright eerie.

Each chapter unravels a unique story, a distinct footprint in the vast wilderness of the unknown.

As we move deeper into the book, we encounter tales that might seem outlandish at first glance. The "Manchester Pusher", a spectral figure associated with canal deaths in Manchester, or the Northumberland Hairy Haggis, a creature more at home in a fantasy novel than in the English countryside. Yet these stories are part of local lore, adding rich layers to our understanding of these regions.

We also delve into stories of large cats prowling the UK countryside - from Bodmin to Exmoor and beyond. These tales challenge our understanding of what's possible and remind us that nature can still surprise us.

The book also pays homage to folklore creatures like The Welsh Dragon and The Selkies of Orkney. These mythical beings may not have physical evidence to back their existence, but they hold cultural significance and continue to inspire awe and wonder.

In essence, this book is an invitation to suspend disbelief, to entertain the implausible, and to journey into the heart of the UK's most enduring mysteries. It's about celebrating the unknown and cherishing the thrill that comes with it. So, come along on this extraordinary journey - who knows what we might encounter on these strange and shadowy paths?

Chapter 1: The Loch Ness Monster

The Loch Ness Monster, also known as "Nessie," is a legendary creature that is said to inhabit Loch Ness, a large freshwater loch in the Scottish Highlands. The creature is typically described as a large, long-necked, aquatic animal with humps that protrude from the water. The legend of Nessie has captured the imaginations of people around the world, and the creature has become one of the most famous cryptids of all time.

Sightings of the Loch Ness Monster date back to the 6th century, with the first modern sighting reported in 1933 by a couple who claimed to have seen an enormous creature crossing the road in front of them. Since then, there have been hundreds of reported sightings, photographs, and videos of Nessie, as well as several scientific expeditions and studies aimed at discovering the truth behind the legend.

Despite the widespread interest and investigation, the existence of the Loch Ness Monster remains unproven. Sceptics argue that many reported sightings can be explained as hoaxes, misidentifications of known animals, or natural phenomena, while believers point to the large number of credible eyewitness accounts and unexplained evidence as proof of the creature's existence.

One of the most famous pieces of evidence for the existence of Nessie is the Loch Ness Monster photograph taken in 1934 by Robert Wilson. The photograph shows a dark shape in the water with a long neck and head, which many people believe to be the creature. However, the photograph has been widely criticized for being blurry and ambiguous, and some researchers have suggested that it could be a hoax.

Since then, there have been numerous other photographs, videos, and sonar scans that have been touted as evidence of Nessie's existence, but none have been conclusively proven. Scientific investigations into the loch have also failed to find any evidence of a large, unknown creature living in its waters.

Despite the lack of conclusive evidence, the legend of the Loch Ness Monster continues to attract visitors to the loch, with many people hoping to catch a glimpse of the elusive creature. The area around Loch Ness has become a popular tourist destination, with numerous shops, hotels, and attractions dedicated to the legend of Nessie.

Theories about the identity of the Loch Ness Monster range from the mundane to the fantastical. Some researchers have suggested that the creature could be a large eel after a DNA study was done on the water of Loch Ness in 2018 and discovered high quantities of eel DNA, while others have proposed that it is a type of prehistoric reptile that has somehow survived into the present day. Still, others have suggested that the creature could be a type of undiscovered animal or even a supernatural being.

Despite the many sightings and investigations over the years, the mystery of the Loch Ness Monster remains unsolved. Whether Nessie is a real creature or simply a myth, the legend of the monster has captured the imaginations of people around the world and continues to inspire curiosity and wonder.

Chapter 2: The Owlman of Mawnan

The Owlman of Mawnan is a cryptid that has been reported in the Mawnan area of Cornwall, in the south-west of England. The creature is described as being a humanoid figure with wings and large, owl-like eyes.

The first reported sighting of the Owlman of Mawnan occurred in April 1976, when two young girls were walking through the woods near Mawnan Old Church. They claimed to have seen a large, feathered creature that had glowing eyes and wings like an owl. The creature reportedly flew away after a few moments, leaving the girls terrified and shaken.

Over the years, there have been several other reported sightings of the Owlman of Mawnan, with witnesses describing the creature as being around six feet tall with wings that spanned up to ten feet across. Some witnesses have also claimed that the creature emits a strange, humming noise when it is nearby.

Despite the numerous reported sightings, there has been little concrete evidence to support the existence of the Owlman of Mawnan. However, some researchers have suggested that the creature may be a type of giant owl that has been misidentified by witnesses.

The legend of the Owlman of Mawnan has captured the imagination of people around the world, and the creature has become a popular subject of paranormal research and investigation. Some researchers have even suggested that the creature may be linked to other supernatural phenomena that have been reported in the Mawnan area, including sightings of ghostly apparitions and mysterious lights in the sky.

While the true identity of the Owlman of Mawnan may never be known for certain, the legend of the creature continues to fascinate and intrigue people around the world. Whether the creature is a real, flesh-and-blood entity or simply a product of local folklore and legend, it remains one of the most enduring mysteries of the UK's paranormal landscape.

Chapter 3: The Lincolnshire Lizard

The Lincolnshire Lizard is a cryptid that has been reported in the Lincolnshire area of eastern England. The creature is described as being a large, green or grey lizard-like animal, similar in appearance to a monitor lizard or iguana.

Reports of sightings of the Lincolnshire Lizard date back to the 1990s, with numerous witnesses claiming to have seen the creature sunbathing in fields or darting across roads. Some witnesses have described the creature as being up to four feet long, with a long tail and scaly skin.

Despite numerous sightings, no concrete evidence of the Lincolnshire Lizard has ever been found. However, several photographs and videos have been taken over the years that are purported to show the creature, although these have been dismissed by many as hoaxes or misidentifications.

Some scientists have hypothesised that the Lincolnshire Lizard could be a colony of extinct reptiles from the distant past, such plesiosaurs or mosasaurs, that have somehow persisted into the present. Others have suggested that the animal could be a hybrid of various reptile species, or possibly a brand-new, unidentified species.

Despite ongoing investigations by researchers and enthusiasts, the true identity of the Lincolnshire Lizard remains a mystery. However, the legend of the creature has become firmly established in the folklore and mythology of the Lincolnshire area, and sightings of the creature continue to be reported to this day.

The Lincolnshire Lizard has also become the subject of numerous books, documentaries, and films, and has inspired countless debates and discussions about the possibility of undiscovered species living in the UK's wilderness areas. The creature remains a popular subject of interest for cryptozoologists and enthusiasts of the paranormal and unexplained.

Chapter 4: The "Manchester Pusher"

More of a myth than a cryptid, the "Manchester Pusher" is the name given to an unidentified serial killer who is believed to be responsible for a series of deaths in the canals of Manchester, England. The nickname comes from the suspicion that the killer may be pushing his victims into the water to drown.

The first recorded incident occurred in 2008, with the body of 32-year-old furniture maker Anthony Grainger being found in the Bridgewater Canal. Since then, there have been over 80 reported cases of bodies being found in Manchester's waterways, leading to speculation that there may be a serial killer operating in the area.

However, the idea of a serial killer known as the "Manchester Pusher" has been disputed by some. Manchester police have repeatedly stated that there is no evidence of foul play in the majority of the cases, and that the deaths are likely the result of accidents, suicides, or drug and alcohol-related incidents.

Despite this, the speculation surrounding the "Manchester Pusher" continues to persist, with many people convinced that there is a killer on the loose. Some have even suggested that the "Pusher" may be a police officer, due to the high number of incidents and the apparent lack of progress in the investigations.

Various theories have been put forward to explain the deaths, including the possibility that some victims may have been targeted by muggers or attackers who then disposed of their bodies in the canals. Others have suggested that the deaths may be linked to the large number of bars and nightclubs in the area, and the potential for people to fall into the water while under the influence of alcohol.

The speculation surrounding the "Manchester Pusher" has sparked numerous investigations and appeals for information from the public. Manchester police have urged people to remain vigilant when walking near the canals and to take precautions to avoid falling into the water.

The mystery of the "Manchester Pusher" continues to capture the public imagination, with many people fascinated by the possibility of a serial killer operating in their midst. However, until concrete evidence is found, the true identity and motives of the "Pusher" remain unknown.

Chapter 5: Bownessie

"Bownessie" is the nickname given to an unidentified creature said to inhabit Lake Windermere in the Lake District of England. Described as a large, serpentine creature with humps, a long neck and a head resembling that of a plesiosaur, Bownessie has become a popular topic of discussion among cryptozoology enthusiasts and lake visitors.

The first reported sighting of Bownessie occurred in 2006, when a local woman named Shelley Kearney claimed to have seen a large creature in the lake. She reported seeing a dark, humped figure moving through the water near Belle Isle, an island in the centre of the lake. Other sightings followed, with some witnesses claiming to have seen the creature raise its head out of the water or swim near their boats.

Despite the numerous reported sightings, no definitive evidence of Bownessie's existence has been found. Some researchers have suggested that the creature may be a large eel or other type of aquatic animal, while others believe that it may be a hoax perpetuated by people looking to attract tourists to the area.

In 2009, a group of researchers from the Center for Fortean Zoology conducted an investigation into the Bownessie phenomenon. They interviewed witnesses, searched the lake with underwater cameras and sonar equipment, and analysed samples of lake water. However, they were unable to find any conclusive evidence of the creature's existence.

Despite the lack of hard evidence, Bownessie continues to be a popular topic of discussion and speculation among visitors to Lake Windermere. The creature has even inspired a range of merchandise, including T-shirts, mugs and postcards. While the true identity of Bownessie may never be known, the mystery and intrigue surrounding the creature continue to capture the imaginations of people around the world.

Chapter 6: Morgawr

The Cornish Sea Serpent, also known as Morgawr, is a legendary sea creature that is said to inhabit the waters around the coast of Cornwall in southwest England. Descriptions of the creature vary, but it is generally described as a large, serpentine creature, with some reports suggesting it may be up to 60 feet long.

Reports of Morgawr date back to the early 1900s, but it was not until the 1970s that sightings of the creature began to attract serious attention. In 1975, two young boys reported seeing a large creature in Falmouth Bay that they described as being like a crocodile. This was followed by a number of other sightings over the years, including reports of a long, snake-like creature swimming in the waters near Penzance and the Lizard Peninsula.

The most famous sighting of Morgawr occurred in 1976, when a woman named Sheila Bird and her two children claimed to have seen a large, hump-backed creature swimming in the waters off Falmouth. The encounter lasted for several minutes, and the family was able to take photographs of the creature, which were later analysed by experts. The photographs were inconclusive, and while some experts suggested that they may have captured an unknown creature, others dismissed them as hoaxes.

In spite of the numerous reports of Morgawr sightings, the creature's existence is not supported by any hard evidence. Researchers have offered many explanations for the sightings, including the possibility that they represent false identifications of well-known species such as seals or dolphins, while others believe they could be the product of hoaxes or simple misunderstandings.

The legend of Morgawr has inspired a great deal of interest among cryptozoologists and enthusiasts of the paranormal.

Some have suggested that the creature may be related to other sea monsters, such as the Loch Ness Monster in Scotland, while others believe that it may be an undiscovered species of marine animal.

In recent years, sightings of Morgawr have become less common, leading some to suggest that the creature may no longer be living in the waters around Cornwall. However, the legend of the Cornish Sea Serpent continues to capture the imaginations of people around the world, and the possibility of a new discovery in the waters of the southwest coast of England remains an intriguing prospect.

Chapter 7: UK Big Cats

There have been many reports of big cat sightings in the UK over the years, many of which we will focus on in more detail over the next few chapters. While many of these sightings are likely misidentifications of known animals or hoaxes, there are also numerous credible reports that suggest the presence of large, unidentified cats roaming the British countryside.

One of the most famous big cat sightings in the UK occurred in 1980, when a farmer in Shropshire reported seeing a large, black cat-like creature in his fields. The animal was described as being around five feet long with a long tail, and it was reportedly capable of leaping over fences with ease. The sighting sparked a media frenzy, with numerous other reports of similar sightings coming in from across the region.

Another notable big cat sighting in the UK occurred in 1991, when a couple driving through the countryside in Devon claimed to have seen a large, black cat-like animal cross the road in front of them. The animal was described as being around three feet tall with a long tail and muscular body, and it was said to move with incredible speed and agility.

Since then, there have been numerous other big cat sightings reported throughout the UK, including in Wales, Scotland, and other parts of England. In many cases, witnesses describe seeing large, black cats that are similar in appearance to panthers or pumas, while others report seeing more exotic-looking cats with distinctive markings or colours.

Despite the large number of reported sightings, the existence of big cats in the UK remains controversial. Some experts believe that the sightings are simply the result of misidentification or hoaxes, while others argue that there is evidence to suggest that there are indeed large cats living wild in the British countryside.

One theory is that many of these big cats are escaped or released exotic pets, such as panthers or pumas, that have managed to survive and breed in the wild. Another possibility is that the animals are wildcats that have somehow managed to survive in the UK despite being officially declared extinct in the region.

There have been several studies and investigations into the phenomenon of big cat sightings in the UK, including a 1995 government inquiry that concluded that there was no evidence to suggest the existence of a breeding population of big cats in the UK. However, many people remain convinced that the sightings are genuine, and the mystery of the UK's big cats continues to capture the imaginations of people around the world.

Chapter 8: The Beast Of Bodmin

The Beast of Bodmin is one of the most famous of the big cat sightings in the UK, and refers to a large, wild cat-like creature that is said to roam the countryside around the town of Bodmin in Cornwall.

The first recorded sightings of the Beast of Bodmin occurred in the early 1980s, when local farmers and residents began reporting seeing a large, black cat-like animal in the area. The creature was described as being around four feet long with a long tail and muscular build, and it was said to move with incredible speed and agility.

Over the years, there have been numerous sightings of the Beast of Bodmin, with witnesses describing the animal as looking similar to a panther or puma. In many cases, witnesses have reported seeing the creature at night, with some claiming to have heard it growling or snarling in the darkness.

Although several sightings have been claimed, there isn't any conclusive proof that the Beast of Bodmin actually exists. However, a government investigation into the phenomena in 1995 came to the conclusion that there was sufficient evidence to hypothesise the existence of a sizable wild cat in the Bodmin region.

Since then, there have been several high-profile attempts to capture or photograph the Beast of Bodmin. In 1997, a group of researchers set up a series of camera traps in the area in an attempt to capture photographic evidence of the creature. While the cameras did not capture any images of the Beast of Bodmin, they did capture images of several other large animals, including deer and badgers.

In 2013, a group of scientists from the University of Oxford conducted a DNA analysis of several hairs that were reportedly found on a fence post near Bodmin. The analysis suggested that the hairs may have come from a member of the cat family, although it was not possible to determine whether the animal was a domestic cat or something larger.

The Beast of Bodmin's identity may never be determined for sure, but the mythology of the beast endures, with new reports of sightings and tales surfacing every year. One of the most lasting mysteries of the UK's natural world, regardless of whether the creature is real or just a creation of local mythology.

Chapter 9: The Beast Of Exmoor

The Beast of Exmoor is a creature described as being a large, black or dark brown, half feline, half canine creature, similar in appearance to a panther or puma.

Reports of sightings of the Beast of Exmoor date back to the 1970s, with numerous witnesses claiming to have seen the creature stalking through the countryside or attacking livestock. Some witnesses have described the creature as being up to eight feet long, with a muscular build and sharp, powerful claws.

In spite of countless sightings, no tangible evidence of the Beast of Exmoor has ever been established. Several images and videos purporting to reveal the monster have been taken throughout the years, however these have been disregarded by many as hoaxes or misidentifications.

Some researchers have suggested that the Beast of Exmoor may be a surviving population of exotic big cats, such as panthers or pumas, that were brought to the UK by wealthy landowners in the early 20th century and then released into the wild when they became too difficult to handle. Others have suggested that the creature may be a hybrid of different big cat species, or even a completely new, undiscovered species.

Despite ongoing investigations by researchers and enthusiasts, the true identity of the Beast of Exmoor remains a mystery. However, the legend of the creature has become firmly established in the folklore and mythology of the Exmoor area, and sightings of the creature continue to be reported to this day.

The Beast of Exmoor has also become the subject of numerous books, documentaries, and films, and has inspired countless debates and discussions about the possibility of undiscovered species living in the UK's wilderness areas.

Chapter 10: The Beast Of Dean

The creature known as the Beast of Dean, also referred to as the Moose-Pig, is a reported cryptid that is said to resemble a wild boar, specifically the Sus scrofa species, but of unusually large size. It is frequently sighted in Gloucestershire, located in the southwestern part of the United Kingdom. The Royal Forest of Dean became a prominent area for sightings starting in 1802, when locals began reporting the presence of an exceptionally large wild boar. There were occasional accounts of fallen trees, crushed hedges and fences, and a purportedly otherworldly roar. Eventually, hunters from the village of Parkend, Gloucestershire managed to capture and kill the creature. Upon examination, the hunters unanimously agreed that the animal they had encountered was unlike any boar or indigenous species they were familiar with. This revelation in March 1807 put an end to the sightings for nearly two centuries. During this period, residents frequently heard a deep, guttural noise in the woods between Parkend and the nearby village of Bream, Gloucestershire.

Among the locals, speculation arose about the possibility of another beast roaming the woodland of the Forest of Dean. However, it wasn't until 1998 that this notion gained some support. In that year, two locals named James Nash and Marshall Davies reported an incident while passing through the woodland between Parkend and Bream. They described an eerie silence in the woods, suddenly disrupted by a low sound that gradually grew louder. As they listened, they heard the rustling of leaves and saw a large shape approaching them in the darkness. At that moment, they couldn't fully comprehend the size of the creature. Filled with fear, they fled from the beast, running towards the village of Parkend, with the creature in pursuit through the woodland. They finally emerged onto a well-lit road in the centre of the village and came to a stop. As they caught their breath, an "unearthly" roar echoed from the woods behind them, leaving the men terrified and struggling to make sense of what had just occurred.

Chapter 11: The Northumberland Hairy Haggis

The Northumberland Hairy Haggis is a mythical creature that is said to inhabit the wilds of Northumberland, a county in the northeast of England. The creature is said to resemble a haggis, a traditional Scottish dish made from sheep's organs, but with a shaggy coat of fur or hair.

The legend of the Northumberland Hairy Haggis is believed to have originated in the 1990s, when a local radio station in the area received a number of reports of sightings of a strange, hairy creature. The creature was said to be about the size of a small dog and had a long, bushy tail and short, stumpy legs.

The legend quickly gained popularity in the region, and the Northumberland Hairy Haggis became something of a cultural icon. It has been featured in a number of local events, including a Hairy Haggis Hunt and a Hairy Haggis Festival, which celebrates the legend with music, food, and drink.

While the Northumberland Hairy Haggis is not a real animal, it has become an important part of the folklore and culture of Northumberland. The legend is often used to promote tourism in the area and is seen as a way to celebrate the unique character of the region.

In recent years, there have been renewed efforts to promote the Northumberland Hairy Haggis as a symbol of the region. Some have suggested that the creature could be used as a mascot for local sports teams or as a way to promote Northumberland's rich cultural heritage.

Overall, the Northumberland Hairy Haggis is a fun and lighthearted legend that has captured the imagination of people in the region and beyond. While it may not be a real animal, it serves as a way to celebrate the unique culture and character of

Northumberland and has become an important part of the region's folklore.

Chapter 12: The Welsh Dragon

The Welsh dragon is a mythical creature that is a symbol of Wales, a country located in the west of the United Kingdom. The dragon is a prominent feature of Welsh folklore and has been used as a symbol of Welsh identity for centuries.

The Welsh dragon is said to be a fierce and powerful creature, with bright red scales and a long, serpentine body. It is often depicted breathing fire, and its wings are said to create powerful winds when it beats them. In Welsh mythology, the dragon is often associated with royalty and is said to have been a symbol of the ancient Welsh kings.

The legend of the Welsh dragon is believed to have originated in ancient times, possibly with the Celts who inhabited the region before the arrival of the Romans. The dragon was said to be a powerful symbol of strength and protection, and it was believed to bring good luck and fortune to those who were worthy.

In the Middle Ages, the Welsh dragon became an important symbol of Welsh nationalism and resistance against English domination. During the reign of King Henry VII, the Welsh dragon was adopted as a symbol of the Tudor dynasty, which was of Welsh origin. Today, the Welsh dragon remains a symbol of Welsh identity and is often used to represent Wales in sporting events, on flags, and in other official capacities.

One of the most famous legends associated with the Welsh dragon is the story of Lludd and Llefelys, which tells of two brothers who had to deal with the problem of three plagues that were causing havoc in Wales. The first was a scream that caused everyone who heard it to go mad with fear, the second was a terrible epidemic that killed people by the thousands, and the third was a dragon that would appear every year and burn crops and livestock.

 The brothers consulted a wise magician who told them to make a great cauldron of mead and to pour it out on a hill where the dragon would appear. They did so, and the dragon drank the mead until it fell asleep. The brothers then wrapped the dragon in a magical sheet and buried it in a stone coffin under the hill. The scream and the epidemic were dealt with in a similar manner.

In modern times, the Welsh dragon is celebrated in a number of festivals and events throughout Wales. The most famous of these is the National Eisteddfod, a festival of Welsh music, poetry, and culture that is held every year in a different location in Wales. The Welsh dragon is also a popular subject for artists and craftspeople, who create a wide range of Welsh dragon-themed products, from jewellery and clothing to pottery and other decorative items.

Overall, the Welsh dragon is an important part of Welsh folklore and culture, and it remains a powerful symbol of Welsh identity and heritage.

Chapter 13: The Suffolk Panther

The Suffolk Panther is a legendary big cat said to inhabit the English county of Suffolk. The creature has been reported sporadically over the years, with sightings dating back to the early 1980s.

Descriptions of the Suffolk Panther vary, but most witnesses describe a large, black or dark-coloured feline resembling a panther or puma. The creature is said to be around 5 to 6 feet long, with a muscular build and a long, thick tail. Witnesses have reported seeing the animal in a variety of locations, including woodlands, fields, and gardens.

There have been several notable sightings of the Suffolk Panther over the years. In 1983, a woman reported seeing a large black cat-like animal in a field near her home in Stowmarket. She described the creature as being around 5 feet long, with a long tail and piercing green eyes. In 1995, a farmer in nearby Bury St. Edmunds reported seeing a large black panther-like animal attacking his sheep.

The most recent sightings occurred in Bruisyard village, near a bridge, where a witness observed "a huge black 'cat' bigger than a Rottweiler" cross past her car.

"I swear it was a panther!" she added.

Another witness claimed they saw a giant cat on the Easton-Wickham Road several years ago, while another said their spouse was walking dogs in the dark on a back road to Badingham when he noticed a "massive cat's head" in the hedge.

Other suggested sightings have occurred in Leiston, Cransford, Sweffling, and Cratfield, and an image has been captured of a giant paw print in a garden in Earl Soham. Some sightings have even placed the creature close to pop star Ed Sheeran's 16-acre estate near Framlingham.

Police in Suffolk received reports of panther or "mountain lion"-like cat sightings from 2016 to 2019 in Woodbridge, Bury St Edmunds, Eye, Colchester, Lowestoft, and on the B1066, B1113, A1088, A1120, and A1017 highways.

The informant was attacked by a "wild cat" in the Lowestoft sighting on June 27, 2018.

Although there have been numerous and diverse sightings in Suffolk, Norfolk has seen the majority of sightings of huge cats.

The county holds the UK record for big cat sightings, with more people than any other region claiming seeing cats as large as leopards, panthers, and jaguars loping across the county's rural areas, hamlets, and towns, including Norwich's downtown.

In recent years, there have been several alleged sightings of big cats in other parts of the UK, which has led to renewed interest in the legend of the Suffolk Panther. While the existence of the creature remains unproven, the legend of the big cat continues to capture the imagination of those who live in and around Suffolk.

Chapter 14: The Selkies Of Orkney

Selkies, also known as seal people or seal-folk, are creatures from Scottish and Irish folklore. According to legend, selkies are seals that have the ability to shed their skin and transform into human form. In Orkney, an archipelago off the northern coast of Scotland, selkies have played an important role in local folklore for centuries.

In Orkney folklore, selkies are said to live in the sea around the islands. They are often depicted as being beautiful and seductive, with the ability to enchant humans with their singing and dancing. According to legend, if a human manages to capture a selkie's skin while it is in human form, the selkie will be bound to the human and forced to become their spouse.

There are many stories in Orkney folklore that feature selkies. One of the most famous is the story of the farmer and the selkie. In this tale, a farmer captures the skin of a female selkie and forces her to become his wife. The selkie eventually gives birth to several children, but remains unhappy in her human form. One day, she finds her skin and escapes back to the sea, leaving her husband and children behind.

Another famous story is the tale of the selkie and the fisherman. In this story, a fisherman falls in love with a female selkie and marries her. However, after several years, the selkie becomes homesick for the sea and returns to the ocean, leaving her husband and children behind.

While selkies are primarily associated with Orkney and other parts of Scotland, similar creatures can be found in folklore from other parts of the world, such as the mermaids of Irish folklore and the sirens of Greek mythology.

Today, selkies continue to be an important part of Orkney's cultural heritage. The islands are home to a number of festivals and events that celebrate the region's folklore and history, including the Orkney Folk Festival and the Orkney Storytelling Festival. The legend of the selkies is also celebrated in literature, music, and art, with many contemporary artists drawing inspiration from the timeless tales of these magical creatures.

Chapter 15: The Shug Monkey

The Shug Monkey is a cryptid that is said to reside in the forests and moors of Northern England, particularly in the region of County Durham. The creature is said to resemble a large monkey or ape-like creature, with shaggy black fur, a dog-like snout, and bright red eyes that glow in the dark.

The origins of the Shug Monkey legend are unclear, but sightings of the creature have been reported since at least the early 19th century. According to local folklore, the Shug Monkey is a malevolent creature that preys on unsuspecting travellers, particularly children who wander too far from their parents.

There have been numerous reported sightings of the Shug Monkey over the years, although the majority of these have been dismissed as hoaxes or misidentifications of known animals. However, there are some who believe that the Shug Monkey may be a real, undiscovered species of primate that has somehow managed to evade scientific detection.

One of the most famous encounters with the Shug Monkey occurred in 1971, when a family on a camping trip in the Durham Dales reported being chased by a large, black, shaggy creature that matched the description of the Shug Monkey. The family claimed that the creature was incredibly fast and agile, and that it seemed to be actively pursuing them. Eventually, they managed to lose the creature in a nearby stream and escaped unharmed.

Despite numerous reported sightings, there is little scientific evidence to support the existence of the Shug Monkey. Some cryptozoologists speculate that the creature may be a remnant population of an undiscovered primate species that once roamed the forests of Britain, while others believe that it may be a supernatural entity or even a physical manifestation of human fear.

In recent years, interest in the Shug Monkey has increased, with several documentaries and podcasts exploring the legend and investigating alleged sightings. However, as with many cryptids, the truth behind the Shug Monkey remains elusive, and it remains one of England's most enduring mysteries.

Chapter 16: The Fen Tiger

Yet another cat-like creature on our list, the Fen Tiger is said to inhabit the Fens of eastern England, specifically the counties of Cambridgeshire, Lincolnshire, and Norfolk. The Fen Tiger is described as a large, black or brown feline resembling a panther or a puma, with sharp teeth, piercing eyes, and powerful legs.

Sightings of the Fen Tiger have been reported since the early 20th century, with the first recorded sighting occurring in the early 1900s near Ramsey, Cambridgeshire. Since then, numerous sightings have been reported, with the most recent being in the late 1990s.

The origins of the Fen Tiger legend are unclear, with some suggesting that it may be a feral big cat that has escaped from captivity or was released into the wild. Others believe that the Fen Tiger is a remnant population of the prehistoric sabre-toothed tiger, which lived in the area during the Pleistocene epoch.

There have been several reported attacks attributed to the Fen Tiger, although there is little concrete evidence to support these claims. In the 1980s, a farmer in Lincolnshire reported that one of his sheep had been killed by a large, unidentified predator. In the 1990s, a man in Cambridgeshire claimed that he had been chased by a large, black cat while walking his dog.

Despite the numerous reported sightings, there has been little concrete evidence to support the existence of the Fen Tiger. No physical specimens or remains have ever been recovered, and there has been no genetic evidence to suggest that the Fen Tiger is a distinct species. Sceptics argue that the sightings may be the result of misidentification of domestic cats or other animals, or simply hoaxes.

Regardless of its existence, the Fen Tiger remains a popular legend in the Fens of eastern England, with many people convinced of its existence and others dismissing it as a myth.

Chapter 17: The Black Shuck

The Black Shuck is a legendary ghostly black dog that is said to roam the coast and countryside of East Anglia, a region of eastern England. According to folklore, the creature is often depicted as a huge, fierce-looking hound with shaggy black fur, fiery red eyes, and bared teeth.

The name "Black Shuck" may derive from the Old English word "scucca," which means "demon" or "devil." The origins of the legend are unclear, but tales of ghostly black dogs have been a part of English folklore for centuries. The Black Shuck is said to be particularly associated with the area around the Norfolk coast.

According to legend, encounters with the Black Shuck are usually ominous, and the creature is often seen as a harbinger of doom. The beast is said to appear suddenly on dark, stormy nights, and to approach travellers on lonely roads or in isolated places. Those who encounter the Black Shuck are said to be filled with a sense of dread and fear, and the creature is said to be capable of causing death or injury with a single touch.

Over the centuries, there have been many reported sightings of the Black Shuck. One of the most famous occurred in 1577 in the town of Bungay, in Suffolk, when the beast is said to have burst into the church during a violent storm, killing two worshippers and injuring several others. Another famous sighting occurred in the neighbouring town of Blythburgh, where the creature is said to have left scorch marks on the door of the church after it tried to enter.

Despite the many sightings, some historians have suggested that the legend of the Black Shuck may have been embellished over time, and that some of the reports may have been exaggerated or even invented. Nevertheless, the story of the ghostly black dog continues to be a popular part of English folklore, and the Black Shuck remains a potent symbol of fear and foreboding in the popular imagination.

Chapter 18: The Grey Man of Ben MacDhui

The Grey Man of Ben MacDhui is a creature that is said to inhabit the Cairngorm Mountains in Scotland. The Cairngorms are the largest mountain range in the United Kingdom, and Ben MacDhui is the second-highest peak in the range, standing at 1,309 meters (4,295 feet) tall.

The Grey Man is said to be a large, humanoid figure, standing up to ten feet tall, covered in grey or brown hair, and emitting a foul odour. It is said to stalk hikers and climbers in the area, following them silently and causing feelings of dread and fear.

The first recorded sighting of the Grey Man of Ben MacDhui was in 1891 by a climber named Hector Munro. Munro reported feeling as though he was being followed by an unseen presence while descending from the summit of the mountain. He described the sensation as being like "a large man following me, walking in a queer, shuffling manner."

Since Munro's report, many other climbers and hikers have reported similar experiences, often describing the same foul odour and feeling of being stalked. Some have even reported hearing strange, unidentifiable sounds and seeing strange lights on the mountain.

Despite numerous sightings and reports, no concrete evidence of the Grey Man's existence has ever been found. Some scientists speculate that the sightings may be the result of infrasound, a type of sound that is below the range of human hearing but can cause feelings of fear and unease in those who experience it. Others believe that the sightings may be the result of hallucinations caused by the high altitude and extreme physical exertion required to climb the mountain.

Regardless of the cause of the sightings, the legend of the Grey Man of Ben MacDhui has persisted for over a century, and the mountain remains a popular destination for hikers and climbers looking to test their mettle against the unknown.

Chapter 19: The Chupacabra of Fife

The Chupacabra of Fife is a cryptid reportedly sighted in Fife, Scotland. The creature is said to resemble the legendary Chupacabra, which is commonly reported in parts of the Americas, but with some distinct differences. The name "Chupacabra" is Spanish for "goat-sucker," and it is so named because it was first reported to have attacked and killed livestock, especially goats.

In Fife, the creature was first sighted in 2004, when a number of farmers reported finding their sheep dead with strange puncture wounds to their necks. Some of the sheep were also partially eaten, and the farmers were convinced that something unusual was responsible. A local newspaper, The Fife Free Press, reported on the sightings, and soon the story began to attract national and international attention.

The Chupacabra of Fife is described as being around 4 to 5 feet in height and covered in black fur. Its head is said to be similar to that of a dog, but with a much longer snout and sharp teeth. It is said to have large, glowing red eyes, and some witnesses have reported seeing a long, thin tail.

Despite the widespread media attention, no concrete evidence of the Chupacabra of Fife has ever been found. Some sceptics have suggested that the sheep may have been killed by more mundane predators, such as dogs or foxes, and that the puncture wounds were caused by scavengers after the fact. Others have suggested that the sightings may be the result of misidentification, with witnesses mistaking a known animal for something more unusual.

Interestingly, there have been other reported sightings of Chupacabras in Europe, including in Spain and Portugal. These sightings have also been met with scepticism from the scientific community, who have suggested that they may be the result of hysteria and mass suggestion.

Overall, the Chupacabra of Fife remains an intriguing mystery, and its existence, like that of many other cryptids, continues to be debated by cryptozoologists and sceptics alike. Whether the creature is real or not, its legend serves as a reminder of the enduring power of folklore and the human fascination with the unknown.

Chapter 20: The Norfolk Wolfman

The Norfolk Wolfman is a cryptid creature that is said to roam the countryside of Norfolk, England. It is often described as a large, wolf-like creature with shaggy fur, sharp teeth, and glowing red eyes.

Sightings of the Norfolk Wolfman date back to the early 1900s, but it wasn't until the 1970s that the creature gained wider public attention. In 1972, a farmer in the village of Stiffkey reported seeing a large, wolf-like creature attacking his sheep. He claimed that the animal had killed several of his animals, leaving them with deep bite marks and torn throats. The farmer's description of the creature matched that of the Norfolk Wolfman.

Since then, there have been numerous other reported sightings of the creature, with witnesses describing it as a large, wolf-like animal that is often seen hunting in the fields and woods of Norfolk. Some have claimed that the creature is able to stand on its hind legs, giving it a more human-like appearance.

There have also been reports of strange, howling noises coming from the woods at night, which some have attributed to the Norfolk Wolfman. In some cases, witnesses have reported feeling a sense of dread or fear when in the presence of the creature.

Despite the many reported sightings and encounters with the Norfolk Wolfman, there is no concrete evidence to suggest that the creature actually exists. Some sceptics have suggested that the sightings may be the result of misidentification or hoaxing.

However, many locals in Norfolk firmly believe in the existence of the Norfolk Wolfman, and some have even formed groups to search for evidence of the creature's existence.

The legend of the Norfolk Wolfman continues to fascinate and intrigue people to this day.

Chapter 21: The Green Children of Woolpit

The Green Children of Woolpit is an unusual legend originating from the village of Woolpit in Suffolk, England. The legend dates back to the 12th century and tells the story of two children, a brother and sister, who were discovered in a pit by local farmers. The children had green-hued skin and spoke an unknown language. They were taken to the home of a local landowner, Sir Richard de Calne, where they were cared for.

Over time, the girl became accustomed to her new surroundings and began to eat regular food. However, her brother remained sickly and died not long after their discovery. The girl eventually learned to speak English and told her hosts that she and her brother had come from a place called St. Martin's Land, a place where the sun never shone, and everything was always green. She said that they had been tending their father's flock when they had heard a loud noise and suddenly found themselves in a strange land.

The girl's skin lost its green colour over time, and she eventually married a man from King's Lynn. She and her husband lived in the town of Bury St. Edmunds, where she was known as "Agnes Barre." The legend of the Green Children has been passed down through the centuries and has become a popular story in English folklore.

Some theories suggest that the Green Children may have been refugees from a foreign country or that they may have been suffering from a rare medical condition that caused their skin to appear green. Another theory suggests that the children may have been extraterrestrial beings, as their description matches that of some accounts of alien encounters.

However, most historians believe that the Green Children were most likely the children of Flemish immigrants who had settled in the area. The legend may have arisen from a misinterpretation of their clothing, which may have been dyed green, or from the fact that they spoke a foreign language. Nonetheless, the story of the Green Children continues to captivate people's imaginations and remains a popular tale in English folklore.

Chapter 22: The Wiltshire Wyrm

The Wiltshire Wyrm, also known as the Pewsey Wyrm or the Potterne Worm, is a legendary creature said to inhabit the county of Wiltshire in England. The wyrm is described as a giant serpent-like creature with multiple humps or coils and a pair of wings. Its size is said to range from as small as a common adder to as large as a steam engine, with reports of lengths up to 100 feet long.

The earliest recorded sighting of the Wiltshire Wyrm dates back to the 9th century, when a group of monks at a monastery in nearby Wilton reported seeing a large dragon-like creature flying over the town. The creature was said to have red scales and spewed fire from its mouth.

In the centuries that followed, there were numerous reports of a giant serpent-like creature in the area. One of the most famous sightings occurred in the early 17th century when a man named John Aubrey claimed to have seen the creature near the village of Pewsey. Aubrey described the wyrm as being around 3 feet thick with a scaly body and estimated its length to be around 14 feet. He also reported that the creature had small legs and two wings that allowed it to fly short distances.

In 1817, a group of men were digging a ditch near the village of Potterne when they claimed to have uncovered the remains of the Wiltshire Wyrm. The creature was said to be around 60 feet long and had a head that resembled that of a crocodile. However, sceptics have suggested that the remains were likely those of a large snake or a whale.

Despite the lack of physical evidence, reports of the Wiltshire Wyrm have continued into modern times. In the 1960s, a group of schoolchildren reported seeing a large serpent-like creature in a pond near the village of Alton Barnes. In 2012, a man claimed to have spotted the wyrm while walking his dog near Pewsey.

There are several theories as to what the Wiltshire Wyrm could be, ranging from a surviving species of plesiosaur to a misidentified large snake or eel. Others suggest that the creature is purely mythical, and its sightings are simply the result of folklore and legend.

Overall, the Wiltshire Wyrm remains a fascinating and mysterious creature in English folklore, with reported sightings dating back centuries. While there is no concrete evidence to support its existence, the legend of the wyrm continues to capture the imagination of locals and visitors alike.

Chapter 23: The Dobhar-chú

The Dobhar-chú, also known as the King Otter, is a legendary creature from Irish folklore. It is often described as a hybrid creature with features of both a dog and an otter, although some accounts depict it as a cross between a dog and a fish. The Dobhar-chú is primarily associated with water and is believed to have fur with protective properties, although these claims lack substantial evidence due to the nature of the creature's oral tradition.

In terms of physical description, the Dobhar-chú closely resembles an otter but is said to be much larger, approximately five times the size, reaching lengths of around 10 to 15 feet. It is often depicted with a white pelt, black ear tips, and a distinct black cross marking on its back. However, due to the murky waters it is believed to inhabit, the creature's pelt is sometimes portrayed as being darker in colour.

The name "Dobhar-chú" is derived from the Irish language, with "dobhar" being one of several words for "otter" in Irish. The modern Irish word for "water" is "uisce," although "dobhar" is occasionally used. The term "cú" translates to "hound" in Irish, as seen in other Irish mythological figures like Cúchulainn, which means "Culainn's hound." The Dobhar-chú is also referred to by other names such as dobarcu, doyarchu, dhuragoo, dorraghow, or anchu in anglicized versions.

One notable reference to the Dobhar-chú is a headstone found in Conwall cemetery in Glenade, County Leitrim. The headstone depicts the creature and is associated with a local tale of an attack on a woman by the Dobhar-chú. The stone is believed to mark the grave of a woman who was allegedly killed by the creature in the 18th century. The monument itself is a recumbent sandstone slab, approximately 4 ft. 6 ins. by 1 ft. 10 ins., featuring a carving of an animal resembling a dog with distinctive rib depth and strong thighs. The tail is long and curved, displaying a tuft at the end. The relief carvings on the stone depict the lettering and imagery.

One particular account involving the Dobhar-chú tells the story of Grace McGloighlin, also known as Grace Connolly, who lived in Creevelea, located at the northwest corner of Glenade Lough in 1722. According to various versions of the tale, Grace went down to the lough to wash clothes one morning. Some say her husband, Terrence, rushed to the shore upon hearing her screams, while others state that he went in search of her when she did not return that evening. In both versions, Mr. McGloighlin discovered her mutilated body with the Dobhar-chú sleeping on top of her. Terrence quickly returned home, grabbed a dagger, and went back to confront and kill the creature. As the Dobhar-chú perished, it emitted a whistling yell to its mate, which rose from the lough. Terrence engaged in a long and bloody battle with the second Dobhar-chú, with some accounts suggesting he had assistance, ultimately emerging victorious.

These accounts and legends surrounding the Dobhar-chú have been passed down through generations, adding to the rich tapestry of Irish folklore and mythology.

Chapter 24: The Benbecula Mermaid

In 1830, a group of individuals were diligently cutting seaweed on the West Coast of the picturesque Island of Benbecula. Engaged in their work, they suddenly witnessed a remarkable sight. A few yards away in the water, a peculiar creature caught their attention, prompting one woman to cry out in astonishment. This creature, resembling a diminutive woman, defied any previous encounters the beachgoers had experienced. Filled with alarm and curiosity, the men of the group bravely ventured into the water, attempting to capture the mysterious being. However, their efforts were in vain as the creature skilfully eluded their grasp. In a desperate act, a young boy hurled a rock with all his might, striking the creature on the back of her head. Emitting a cry of pain, she vanished beneath the waves, leaving the onlookers bewildered.

Several days later, a lifeless form washed ashore on the beach at Culle Bay, a picturesque stretch of coastline located near the township of Nunton, a few miles north of the initial sighting. This creature displayed an upper body reminiscent of a fully developed woman, yet possessed the stature of a mere four-year-old girl. Her appearance was defined by cascading tresses of dark, glossy hair and a pallid complexion. The lower half of her body bore resemblance to a salmon, although devoid of its characteristic scales.

News of this mysterious creature swiftly spread, captivating the attention of crowds who flocked to the beach, eager to catch a glimpse of the extraordinary find. Without exception, each witness concurred that they were in the presence of a mermaid. The local sheriff, acting as the representative of MacDonald of Clanranald, was summoned to the scene. Upon witnessing the creature, he validated its classification as a mermaid. To honour the strange being, he called for a coffin and shroud to be transported to the beach. With solemn reverence, the creature was placed within the confines of the coffin and subsequently interred in a nearby churchyard. The mermaid's funeral is said to have drawn one of the largest and most attentive crowds ever witnessed on the island, with proceedings meticulously adhering to the customs of a proper Christian burial.

Curiously, no grave marker associated with the incident was identified within the church grounds, leading many to speculate that the creature was laid to rest near the dunes instead. A recent survey of a substantial stone located at the southern end of the bay aimed to determine whether it might serve as the mermaid's final resting place. Regrettably, the results of the investigation proved inconclusive, leaving the mystery unresolved.

Benbecula has yielded numerous accounts of mermaid encounters throughout its history. Colin Campbell, a diligent crofter hailing from Barra, found himself involved in a captivating incident. Initially mistaking a fishing otter for his quarry, he prepared to take aim and shoot. However, curiosity prevailed, and he decided to observe the creature through his telescope instead. To his astonishment, he beheld what appeared to be a woman cradling a small baby in her arms. The mermaid caught sight of him standing on the shore and promptly vanished, leaving Campbell in a state of incredulity.

These tales of mermaid encounters, interwoven with the folklore of Benbecula, continue to captivate the imagination. Passed down through generations, they provide a glimpse into the enigmatic realm of merfolk, leaving a lasting impression on the collective memory of the island's inhabitants and visitors alike.

Chapter 25: The Sussex Serpent

The serene coastal town of Sussex, nestled along the southern shores of England, is known for its picturesque landscapes and charming villages. But beyond its postcard-perfect façade lies a mystery that has both captivated and perplexed the locals for generations - the legend of the Sussex Serpent.

In the late 18th century, reports of an enormous sea serpent lurking off the Sussex coast began to surface. Eyewitness accounts spoke of a creature with a serpentine body, adorned with glistening scales, and a head that rose dramatically from the water. Some claimed it had a crown-like crest, while others described it as having menacing, glowing eyes that could pierce the darkest of nights.

The sightings were not confined to a single location. Reports of the Sussex Serpent emerged from various coastal towns along the English Channel, creating a sense of awe and trepidation among the coastal communities. Fishermen, sailors, and residents alike shared their encounters with this elusive creature.

One particularly chilling account tells of a local fisherman who, while out at sea one misty morning, found himself face to face with the monstrous serpent. According to his testimony, the creature's head, the size of a small boat, emerged from the water, its eyes fixated on him with an otherworldly intensity. Frozen with fear, the fisherman watched as the serpent gracefully glided beneath the surface, disappearing into the depths.

As rumours and sightings spread, scientific minds turned their attention to the phenomenon. Scholars and naturalists launched investigations, hoping to unveil the truth behind the Sussex Serpent. Some proposed that it was a surviving species of prehistoric marine reptile, while others believed it was an undiscovered species of giant eel or sea serpent.

Despite efforts to capture or document the creature, the Sussex Serpent remained an enigma. Sceptics dismissed the sightings as hoaxes or exaggerations, while believers held steadfast to their accounts. The mystery of the Sussex Serpent continues to endure, captivating the imaginations of residents and drawing curious visitors to the serene shores of Sussex.

Chapter 26: The Peak District Mothman

High in the rolling hills of England's Peak District, a place known for its stunning natural beauty and peaceful surroundings, an unsettling phenomenon took hold that sent shivers down the spines of those who encountered it - the legend of the Peak District Mothman.

The story of the Peak District Mothman begins in the late 1960s when residents of the small towns and villages surrounding the Peak District National Park reported sightings of a bizarre and eerie creature. Described as a tall, dark figure with enormous wings and piercing red eyes, this enigmatic being would often appear at twilight, casting an ominous shadow over the tranquil landscape.

One of the most notable encounters occurred in 1966 when two young couples were driving through the winding roads of the Peak District on a moonlit night. As they rounded a bend, their headlights illuminated a grotesque figure standing on the side of the road. It had wings folded against its back, and its red eyes seemed to glow with an unnatural malevolence. Terrified, the witnesses sped away, but the image of the Mothman haunted their dreams for years to come.

Word of the Peak District Mothman spread quickly, and more reports poured in from various locations within the national park. Witnesses claimed the creature was not aggressive but rather seemed to be a foreboding omen, a harbinger of disaster. Some even speculated that its appearances were linked to tragic events that occurred in the region.

One account that fuelled the legend involved a local farmer who, after encountering the Mothman in the vicinity of his farm, suffered a series of inexplicable misfortunes, including the mysterious deaths of his livestock and the unexplained collapse of his barn. While sceptics attributed these incidents to mere coincidence, the farmer and many others in the community believed the creature had brought a curse upon him.

In the years that followed, the Peak District Mothman sightings gradually dwindled, leaving behind a legacy of mystery and intrigue. Sceptics dismissed the accounts as mere hallucinations or hoaxes, while believers pondered the possibility of a supernatural entity haunting the serene wilderness of the Peak District.

One compelling aspect of this cryptid's story is the psychological and cultural impact it had on the witnesses and the local community. The Mothman became a symbol of the unknown, a dark enigma that challenged the boundaries of human understanding. Folklore and legends often thrive in areas where the natural world meets the supernatural, and the Peak District Mothman was no exception.

Local authorities and investigators attempted to unravel the mystery. They interviewed witnesses, examined physical evidence, and scoured the surrounding wilderness in search of clues. However, no conclusive evidence was ever found to definitively prove or disprove the existence of the Mothman.

Some experts speculated that the Peak District Mothman could have been a misidentification of known wildlife, such as owls or large birds of prey, in dim light or foggy conditions. Others suggested that it might have been a manifestation of collective anxiety or fear, fuelled by the turbulent social and political climate of the 1960s.

Yet, the legend persisted, and the Mothman continued to be a topic of discussion among locals and visitors alike. The story of the creature was passed down through generations, becoming an enduring part of the Peak District's folklore.

As we reflect on the legend of the Peak District Mothman, it raises intriguing questions about the human fascination with the mysterious and the uncanny. Why do such legends persist, even in the face of scepticism and scientific inquiry? What does the story of the Mothman reveal about the relationship between the human imagination and the natural world?

While we may never have definitive answers about the Peak District Mothman, one thing is clear - the legend endures, a testament to the enduring power of folklore and the enduring allure of the unknown. The Mothman's red eyes still seem to watch over the tranquil landscape of the Peak District, a reminder that, in the shadowy corners of our world, mysteries continue to beckon, waiting to be explored by those brave enough to seek them out.

Chapter 27: The Galloway Princess

The Galloway Princess is a legend that has emerged in the Galloway region of Scotland. It is said to be the ghostly apparition of a woman who was killed in a carriage accident. The story goes that a young woman was travelling in a carriage on the road between Kirkcudbright and Gatehouse of Fleet, when the carriage was involved in a terrible accident. The woman was killed instantly, and her body was thrown into the nearby river.

Since then, there have been numerous reports of a ghostly figure, said to be that of the young woman, walking along the riverbank. According to the legend, she appears as a beautiful young woman, dressed in a long white gown. Some people have even reported seeing her riding in a ghostly carriage, pulled by four white horses.

There have also been reports of strange occurrences on the stretch of road where the accident is said to have occurred. Some drivers have reported feeling as if they were being watched, while others have reported hearing strange noises or seeing unusual lights. It is not clear whether these incidents are related to the Galloway Princess or are simply the result of the imagination of those who have heard the legend.

The legend of the Galloway Princess has been passed down through the generations and is still widely known in the region today. Some people believe that the ghost of the young woman still haunts the area and that her spirit will never find rest until she has been given a proper burial. Others see the story as simply a local legend, passed down over time and embellished with each retelling. Whatever the truth behind the legend, the Galloway Princess remains a popular tale in the folklore of Scotland.

Chapter 28: The Ayrshire Banshee

Scotland, with its rich history of folklore and legends, is no stranger to tales of the supernatural. Among these, the Ayrshire Banshee holds a particularly eerie and mournful place. Often associated with foretelling death, the Banshee is a ghostly figure whose wailing cries are believed to herald the impending demise of a family member.

The Ayrshire Banshee is unique in that it has been associated with a specific lineage—the Kennedy family. The Kennedys, an ancient Scottish clan, were known for their power and influence in the region. However, with great power often comes great tragedy, and the Kennedys were no exception.

The legend of the Ayrshire Banshee dates back centuries, with tales of the ghostly figure appearing to Kennedy clan members in their darkest hours. Her appearance was said to be a warning—a harbinger of death to come. Witnesses described her as a tall, ethereal woman, dressed in flowing white garments, her long hair blowing in an otherworldly breeze. Her eyes, however, were where the true terror lay. They glowed with an eerie, phosphorescent light that pierced the darkest of nights.

One of the most well-known accounts of the Ayrshire Banshee's presence occurred in the 16th century. As the story goes, the head of the Kennedy clan at that time was Sir John Kennedy of Culzean Castle. He was a powerful and respected figure, but his family was not immune to the tragedies that befell so many noble houses in Scotland.

One fateful night, as Sir John and his family gathered in the candlelit halls of Culzean Castle, the mournful wail of the Banshee filled the air. Her eerie cry echoed through the corridors, chilling the hearts of all who heard it. Terrified, the Kennedys knew that the Banshee's visit foretold a death within their family.

Days later, news arrived that Sir John's son, a valiant knight, had perished in a distant battle. The Banshee's warning had come to pass, and the Kennedy clan was plunged into mourning.

The legend of the Ayrshire Banshee persisted over the centuries, with countless reports of her appearances before Kennedy family deaths. It became a solemn tradition within the clan—a reminder of their enduring connection to the supernatural and the inexorable march of time.

Sceptics have attempted to rationalize the sightings of the Ayrshire Banshee, suggesting that these eerie apparitions may have been the result of grief and superstition rather than actual supernatural events. In times of great sorrow, the mind can play tricks, and even the most rational individuals may interpret ordinary sounds and occurrences as harbingers of doom.

Yet, for the Kennedy clan, the legend of the Ayrshire Banshee was more than a mere superstition; it was a deeply ingrained part of their heritage and history.

In recent years, as the Kennedy clan's influence waned, the tales of the Ayrshire Banshee began to fade into obscurity. The modern world seemed less inclined to believe in the supernatural, and the old traditions and legends lost their grip on the collective imagination.

Nevertheless, the legend of the Ayrshire Banshee serves as a poignant reminder of the enduring power of folklore and the profound impact it can have on those who believe.

Chapter 29: The Hertfordshire Hare Man

In the quiet and picturesque county of Hertfordshire, nestled in the heart of England, there exists a peculiar legend—one that combines the worlds of man and beast in a truly enigmatic fashion. This is the tale of the Hertfordshire Hare Man.

The Hertfordshire Hare Man is a cryptid figure that has long intrigued the local population, blending elements of the natural world with the supernatural. Described as a creature with the body of a man and the head of a hare, it's a strange and unsettling hybrid that has left many baffled and curious.

The legend of the Hertfordshire Hare Man dates back for generations, with sightings and stories passed down through the years. Witnesses describe this creature as standing upright on two legs, with a humanoid body, but its head is unmistakably that of a hare, complete with long ears and large, expressive eyes. Its fur, they say, is a patchwork of earthy brown and grey tones, allowing it to blend seamlessly with the woodland surroundings.

Many accounts of the Hare Man suggest that it's a solitary and elusive creature, often spotted in the dense forests and fields that characterize Hertfordshire. Some witnesses claim to have seen it engaged in seemingly human-like activities, such as foraging for food or tending to an odd assortment of objects gathered in its den.

One particularly intriguing aspect of the Hertfordshire Hare Man legend is the mysterious aura that surrounds it. Locals have reported a deep sense of unease and fascination when encountering this cryptid. Some even believe that it possesses supernatural abilities, able to move silently through the forest and vanish without a trace.

As with many cryptid legends, scepticism abounds. Critics argue that the Hertfordshire Hare Man is likely a case of misidentification, with witnesses mistaking ordinary animals, such as hares or deer, for this peculiar creature. The power of suggestion, they say, can play tricks on the mind, transforming the familiar into something altogether more mysterious.

Nevertheless, the legend of the Hertfordshire Hare Man persists, passed down through generations as a quirky and enigmatic part of local folklore. It serves as a reminder that even in our modern age, when science and reason often prevail, there are corners of the world where mystery and the supernatural continue to captivate our imagination.

In recent years, as Hertfordshire has evolved into a bustling suburban region, the Hare Man sightings have become less frequent. The demands of urban life seem to have pushed this cryptid further into the realm of legend, a relic of a time when the natural world and the supernatural were intertwined in the minds of those who called this county home.

Whether it's a creature of myth or a misunderstood denizen of the woods, the Hertfordshire Hare Man remains a fascinating enigma, forever etched into the annals of local folklore.

Chapter 30: The Lancashire Boggart

In the heart of Lancashire, a county steeped in history and folklore, there exists a legend that has both intrigued and terrified generations—the enigmatic and mischievous creature known as the Lancashire Boggart.

The Lancashire Boggart, often depicted as a shape-shifting and malevolent spirit, has long been a fixture of local tales and superstitions. Its name alone carries an air of mystery, evoking a sense of unease and trepidation in those who have heard of its antics.

Unlike other cryptids or supernatural beings, the Lancashire Boggart doesn't conform to a single, easily recognizable form. Instead, it is said to have the ability to assume various shapes and forms, making it a particularly elusive and unpredictable entity. Witnesses and storytellers have described it as a shadowy figure, an ethereal mist, or even a monstrous creature, depending on the situation and the fears of those who encounter it.

The origins of the Lancashire Boggart are shrouded in mystery, but its presence in local folklore has endured for centuries. It is often associated with rural settings, remote cottages, and ancient woodlands, where it is said to play tricks on unsuspecting residents. These pranks can range from the relatively harmless, like moving household objects or creating eerie sounds, to more sinister deeds, such as causing livestock to fall ill or crops to wither.

One common thread in Lancashire Boggart stories is the notion that it feeds off the fear and unease of humans. It seems to delight in causing chaos and confusion, relishing the emotional turmoil it creates. Some believe that it may even be drawn to places or individuals experiencing heightened levels of stress or anxiety, making it a potentially unwelcome presence during times of hardship.

While sceptics may dismiss Boggart sightings as mere superstition or the result of overactive imaginations, believers insist that their experiences are very real. Tales of encounters with this elusive entity continue to surface, passed down through generations as cautionary tales of the supernatural.

In some instances, residents have gone to great lengths to ward off the Lancashire Boggart. Protective charms, talismans, and rituals have been employed in an effort to keep the mischievous spirit at bay. It is said that iron, salt, and fire are particularly effective deterrents against the Boggart's influence.

As the centuries have passed and Lancashire has evolved from its rural roots into a more urbanized landscape, sightings of the Lancashire Boggart have become increasingly rare. Some attribute this decline to the diminishing connection between modern society and the natural world, suggesting that the Boggart thrived in a time when people were intimately tied to the land and its mysteries.

Nonetheless, the legend of the Lancashire Boggart endures as a reminder of the rich tapestry of folklore that weaves through the history of this region. Whether it is a manifestation of primal fears or a genuine supernatural presence, the Boggart continues to be a source of fascination and fear for those who dwell in Lancashire.

Chapter 31: The Yorkshire Wolds Werewolf

In the remote and windswept landscapes of the Yorkshire Wolds, where rolling hills and vast open spaces stretch as far as the eye can see, an unsettling legend has taken root—a legend that tells of a creature that lurks in the shadows and stalks the moorlands under the light of the full moon. This is the tale of the Yorkshire Wolds Werewolf.

The Yorkshire Wolds, known for their natural beauty and ancient history, are a place where the boundary between the mystical and the mundane can blur, and where centuries-old tales of folklore continue to cast a shadow over the land. Among these tales, the legend of the Yorkshire Wolds Werewolf stands out as a chilling and enduring enigma.

The creature described in the legend is a being capable of transforming from a human form into a monstrous wolf-like creature, often said to be larger and more menacing than an ordinary wolf. Witnesses who have claimed to encounter the Yorkshire Wolds Werewolf describe it as having fur as black as night, eyes that burn with an otherworldly intensity, and a howl that chills the blood.

The legend is steeped in stories of terror and tragedy, often revolving around the creature's rampage through the moorlands under the light of the full moon. Tales of livestock mutilations and eerie nocturnal encounters have been handed down through generations, striking fear into the hearts of those who call the Yorkshire Wolds home.

One of the most unsettling aspects of the Yorkshire Wolds Werewolf legend is the suggestion that it is not merely a creature of the wilderness but can assume human form. Some versions of the tale tell of travellers who encounter a seemingly normal person, only to witness a horrifying transformation into the beastly creature before their very eyes.

Like many cryptid legends, the existence of the Yorkshire Wolds Werewolf is met with scepticism by some who argue that the stories are mere products of superstition, folklore, or the result of misidentifications of known wildlife, particularly large dogs or wolves. However, for those who have had their lives touched by the legend, the fear is all too real.

As the Yorkshire Wolds have evolved from rural landscapes into more populated areas, sightings of the Yorkshire Wolds Werewolf have become increasingly rare. Some suggest that the creature, if it ever existed, may have been driven deeper into the wilderness or that it simply represents a folkloric vestige of a bygone era.

Whether a creature of reality or imagination, the Yorkshire Wolds Werewolf serves as a haunting symbol of the enduring allure of the supernatural and the enigmatic mysteries that continue to captivate our imaginations.

Chapter 32: Spring-heeled Jack

One of the most mysterious and terrifying creatures that haunted the streets of Victorian England was Spring-heeled Jack, a leaping, bounding, fire-breathing fiend that attacked women and men alike. His name came from his ability to jump over walls, roofs, and fences with ease, as if he had springs in his heels. His appearance was equally frightening: he wore a helmet, a cloak, and a tight-fitting white suit that resembled an oilskin. He had clawed hands, glowing red eyes, and a mouth that could spit blue and white flames. He also had a high-pitched laugh and a scream that chilled the blood of his victims.

The first reported sighting of Spring-heeled Jack was in 1837 in London, when a servant girl named Mary Stevens was walking to her employer's house in Lavender Hill after visiting her parents in Battersea. As she crossed Clapham Common, a dark figure suddenly leapt out of a nearby alley and grabbed her. He kissed her face, tore her clothes, and scratched her flesh with his cold and clammy claws. She screamed and struggled, attracting the attention of some passers-by. The assailant then released her and fled into the night with a loud laugh.

The next day, the same figure attacked a coachman who was driving near Mary Stevens' home. He jumped in front of the carriage, causing the horses to panic and the coach to crash. He then escaped by jumping over a nine-foot wall while laughing maniacally.

These incidents were soon followed by more attacks in different parts of London. In February 1838, Jane Alsop heard a knock on the door of her father's house in Bearbind Lane. She opened it and saw a man who claimed to be a police officer. He told her to bring a light, saying that they had caught Spring-heeled Jack in the lane. She brought him a candle, but as soon as she handed it to him, he threw off his cloak and revealed his monstrous form. He spat fire at her face, grabbed her by the neck, and tried to strangle her. She managed to free herself and ran back into the house, but he followed her and attacked her again. Her sister came to her aid and fought him off with a poker. He then ran away, jumping over the garden wall.

A few days later, another young woman named Lucy Scales was walking with her sister in Limehouse after visiting their brother. As they passed Green Dragon Alley, a man stepped out of the shadows and sprayed a jet of fire into Lucy's face, blinding her temporarily. He then fled without harming her further.

These attacks caused a public outcry and panic in London. The Lord Mayor of London, Sir John Cowan, received dozens of letters from people who claimed to have seen or been assaulted by Spring-heeled Jack. He read some of them at a public session at the Mansion House on February 9th 1838. One letter stated that "several respectable persons" had seen Spring-heeled Jack near St John's Wood "in the shape of a bear or some other four-footed animal". Another letter said that "servant girls about Kensington, Hammersmith and Ealing" were afraid to go out at night because of him.

The Lord Mayor expressed his scepticism about the existence of such a creature, but admitted that some of the witnesses were credible and respectable people. He urged the police to investigate the matter seriously and offered a reward for anyone who could capture or identify Spring-heeled Jack.

Many theories were proposed to explain who or what Spring-heeled Jack was. Some people thought he was an escaped lunatic or a prankster with a twisted sense of humour. Others suggested he was a foreign nobleman or an aristocrat with a grudge against society. Some even believed he was a supernatural being or a demon sent by the devil.

One of the main suspects was Henry Beresford, the third Marquess of Waterford, who was known for his wild behaviour and violent temper. He had been involved in several brawls and scandals in London and Ireland, earning him the nickname "the Mad Marquess". He was also said to have a grudge against women after being rejected by one of his love interests. However, there was no conclusive evidence linking him to Spring-heeled Jack, and he died in 1859.

Spring-heeled Jack's reign of terror did not end with London. He was reported to have appeared in many other parts of England throughout the 19th century, especially in the Midlands and the North. He was seen jumping over houses in Sheffield, chasing soldiers in Aldershot, and scaring villagers in Lincolnshire. He was also spotted in Scotland and Wales, where he was sometimes called the "Steel Man" or the "Iron Man" because of his metallic appearance.

The last recorded sighting of Spring-heeled Jack was in 1904 in Liverpool, where he was seen leaping from rooftop to rooftop in Everton. He vanished into the night when some brave residents tried to corner him, and he was never seen again.

The mystery of Spring-heeled Jack remains unsolved to this day. He left behind a legacy of fear and fascination that inspired many works of fiction and folklore. He is considered one of the most enduring and enigmatic legends of the Victorian era.

Chapter 33: The Highgate Vampire

The Highgate Vampire is a name given to a mysterious entity that was reported to haunt the Highgate Cemetery in London, England, in the 1970s. The story began when a local man named David Farrant claimed to have seen a grey figure in the cemetery on Christmas Eve of 1969, and wrote to a newspaper asking if others had witnessed anything similar Soon, several people responded with their own accounts of encountering various ghosts and apparitions in and around the cemetery, such as a tall man in a hat, a woman in white, and a face glaring through the bars of a gate.

However, another man named Sean Manchester challenged Farrant's claim and asserted that the grey figure was actually a vampire, a king of the vampires who had practiced black magic in Romania in the 15th century and had come to England with his followers. Manchester claimed to be an exorcist, a vampire hunter, and a bishop of the Old Catholic Church, and declared that he would destroy the vampire on Friday the 13th of March 1970.

The media frenzy that followed attracted the attention of many curious and adventurous people, who flocked to the cemetery on the night of the hunt, despite the police's attempts to stop them. Some of them were armed with wooden stakes, crosses, and garlic, hoping to catch a glimpse of the vampire or even kill it.

The hunt was unsuccessful, but the story did not end there. In August 1970, the charred and headless remains of a woman's body were found near a catacomb in the cemetery, sparking speculation that it had been used in a black magic ritual or by the vampire itself. Farrant was also arrested in a nearby churchyard with a stake and a crucifix but was later acquitted.

Manchester claimed that he had later found and staked the vampire in its coffin in a vault in the cemetery, with the help of a psychic girl who had been attacked by the vampire. He also claimed that he had burned the remains of another vampire in Crouch End in 1974.

Farrant and Manchester continued to feud over the years, each accusing the other of lying, fraud, and slander. They also wrote books and articles about their experiences and theories, and appeared on various TV shows and documentaries. The Highgate Vampire became one of the most famous and controversial cases of alleged supernatural activity in Britain and inspired many works of fiction and folklore.

Chapter 34: The Cornish Knockers

Beneath the rugged and picturesque landscapes of Cornwall, England, where the rich veins of tin and copper have been mined for centuries, there exists a folklore tradition that tells of an unusual and mystical presence deep within the earth—the mischievous beings known as the Cornish Knockers.

Cornwall, known for its stunning coastline, historic mining heritage, and tales of the supernatural, provides a fitting backdrop for the legends of the Knockers. These legendary creatures have played a unique and fascinating role in the lives of miners who ventured deep underground to extract the treasures of the earth.

The world of Cornish mining was both awe-inspiring and perilous. Miners descended into the dark and labyrinthine tunnels, armed with picks and lanterns, to extract valuable minerals that fuelled the industrial revolution and shaped the region's history. However, the harsh and dangerous conditions of the mines also gave rise to a sense of superstition and wonder, as miners began to attribute strange and unexplained occurrences to the presence of the Knockers.

The Cornish Knockers, also known as Tommyknockers or Bucca, are believed to be diminutive, otherworldly beings, often depicted as small, gnome-like creatures with wrinkled faces and pointed hats. They are said to be a few feet in height, with a mischievous and sometimes benevolent nature.

One of the most distinctive features of the Knockers is their propensity to "knock" on the walls of the mines with their tiny hammers. These rhythmic knocks, which could be heard echoing through the tunnels, were believed to serve as warnings to miners of impending danger, such as cave-ins or gas leaks. Some miners even claimed that the Knockers would helpfully point out the richest seams of ore.

The Knockers, however, were not always helpful. Their mischievous side was often revealed in the form of pranks and tricks played on miners. Tools would mysteriously disappear, candles would be extinguished, and eerie laughter would echo through the tunnels, leaving miners both amused and perplexed.

The folklore of the Cornish Knockers is deeply intertwined with the mining culture of Cornwall. Miners would often leave offerings of food and drink at the entrance of the mines to appease the Knockers and seek their favour. Some believed that angering the Knockers could bring bad luck or misfortune.

The legends of the Knockers endured for generations, passed down through stories and songs, becoming an integral part of Cornish mining heritage. The sense of camaraderie and shared belief in the Knockers created a unique bond among miners, uniting them in both awe and trepidation of the subterranean world they inhabited.

As mining practices evolved and the industrial age progressed, the Knockers gradually faded from the everyday lives of miners. Modernization and technology replaced the traditional practices of the mines, and the Knockers slipped into the realm of legend.

Sceptics have often dismissed the tales of the Knockers as products of superstition and the imagination, attributing the strange occurrences in the mines to natural phenomena, such as echoing sounds or shifting earth. However, for the miners who once toiled beneath the earth, the Knockers were very real and played a significant role in their daily lives.

Chapter 35: The Cumberland Giant

Nestled within the rolling hills and pastoral landscapes of Cumbria, England, lies a legendary tale that has intrigued locals and visitors for centuries—the story of the Cumberland Giant. This colossal figure, said to have once roamed the countryside, has left behind a legacy of awe and wonder.

The legend of the Cumberland Giant is a blend of folklore and historical accounts, with elements of both mystery and marvel. According to the tales passed down through generations, the Giant was an immense figure, towering over the landscape with a stride that covered great distances in a single step. His appearance was said to be formidable, with a rugged and weathered visage that reflected the harshness of the land he called home.

One of the most captivating aspects of the Cumberland Giant legend is the ambiguity surrounding his origins. Some stories suggest that he was a warrior of extraordinary stature, while others attribute his colossal frame to a supernatural or mythical heritage. In either case, the Giant's existence was believed to be a testament to the extraordinary nature of the region.

The Cumberland Giant's exploits were as diverse as the landscapes of Cumbria itself. Tales recount his ability to perform astonishing feats of strength, such as lifting massive boulders and felling entire trees with a single blow. His presence was said to bring both admiration and trepidation, with locals viewing him as both protector and enigma.

One recurring theme in the legend of the Cumberland Giant is his role as a guardian of the land. He was said to watch over the countryside, ensuring the safety and well-being of those who lived there. Some versions of the tale even suggest that he would come to the aid of travellers who found themselves in peril, using his immense strength to rescue them from danger.

The legacy of the Cumberland Giant endures in Cumbrian folklore and the hearts of those who call the region home. Statues and monuments paying tribute to the legendary figure can be found throughout the area, serving as a reminder of the deep connection between myth and reality in this enchanting part of England.

Sceptics have often questioned the veracity of the Cumberland Giant legend, attributing it to the embellishments of storytellers and the exaggerations of historical accounts. They argue that the tales of a colossal figure roaming the countryside are more likely the result of imagination than fact.

Regardless of the Giant's true origins, the legend serves as a testament to the power of storytelling and the enduring fascination with larger-than-life figures who leave an indelible mark on the landscapes they inhabit.

Chapter 36: The Devil's Bridge of Ceredigion

Wales, with its rugged terrain and lush landscapes, is a land steeped in myth and legend. Among its many enigmatic tales, the story of the Devil's Bridge in Ceredigion stands out as a chilling and captivating legend—a story that weaves together a pact with the devil, a bridge that defies natural laws, and a place where folklore and reality collide.

The Devil's Bridge is not a single bridge but a complex of three bridges, each built atop the other, spanning the deep and narrow Mynach Gorge. This architectural marvel, nestled amidst the ancient woodlands of Ceredigion, has drawn travellers, adventurers, and the curious for centuries.

The origins of the Devil's Bridge legend are shrouded in mystery and folklore. According to local tales, the construction of the first bridge was a formidable task, plagued by setbacks and challenges. The bridge would be built during the day, only to mysteriously collapse at night, thwarting the efforts of the builders.

Frustrated and desperate, the villagers of Ceredigion are said to have made a pact with the devil himself. In exchange for completing the bridge, the devil demanded the soul of the first living being to cross it. Reluctantly, the villagers agreed to the diabolical pact.

The Devil's Bridge was swiftly built, but the clever villagers outwitted the devil. Instead of sending a human soul across the bridge, they tempted a dog with a loaf of bread, which lured the animal across first. The devil, furious at being tricked, disappeared into the depths of the gorge, leaving the bridge standing.

Over the centuries, the three bridges were constructed, one atop the other, creating a mesmerizing sight where each bridge spans the gorge below. The oldest bridge, believed to date back to the 11th century, serves as a testament to both human ingenuity and the enduring legacy of the legend.

The Devil's Bridge has captured the imaginations of many poets and artists, inspiring works of literature and paintings that seek to capture its eerie beauty. The sheer depth of the gorge, the lush surroundings, and the haunting atmosphere contribute to the bridge's mystique.

Sceptics have often dismissed the legend of the Devil's Bridge as a product of superstition and folklore, attributing the collapses of early bridges to the challenging terrain and the limitations of medieval engineering. They argue that the pact with the devil is a symbolic explanation for the difficulties faced during construction.

Nonetheless, the Devil's Bridge remains a beloved and enduring symbol of Wales, a place where the mystical and the historical converge. Visitors continue to be drawn to this picturesque location, where the legends of the past linger in the whispers of the trees and the echoes of the Mynach Falls.

Chapter 37: The Lancashire Witches

In the annals of British history, few tales are as chilling and notorious as the story of the Lancashire Witches. These trials, which unfolded in the early 17th century, cast a long shadow over the county of Lancashire, forever associating it with accusations of witchcraft, persecution, and the enduring legacy of superstition.

The Lancashire Witch Trials, which took place between 1612 and 1634, occurred during a time when witch hysteria was at its peak in England. Accusations of witchcraft were alarmingly common, and the authorities, fuelled by fear and religious fervour, were determined to root out and punish those they believed to be witches.

One of the most infamous episodes of the Lancashire Witch Trials involved the Pendle witches, a group of individuals from the area around Pendle Hill. The trials began with the arrest of several women from the Demdike and Chattox families, accused of practicing witchcraft and causing harm to their neighbours.

The accusations against the Pendle witches were chilling and far-reaching. They were said to have consorted with the devil, used charms and curses, and engaged in malevolent acts that brought suffering to those who crossed their paths. The trials that followed were marked by sensational testimonies, confessions under duress, and a climate of fear that permeated the proceedings.

The Pendle witch trials resulted in the execution of ten individuals, including both women and men, who were found guilty of witchcraft and sentenced to death. Their fate serves as a haunting reminder of the hysteria and injustice that characterized this dark chapter in Lancashire's history.

The Lancashire witch trials were not confined to Pendle, as accusations of witchcraft spread to other parts of the county as well. The trials of the Samlesbury witches, the Padiham witches, and the trials in Lancaster further fuelled the hysteria, leading to additional executions and suffering for those accused.

Sceptics and historians have since pointed to the Lancashire witch trials as prime examples of the dangers of mass hysteria, religious extremism, and the persecution of marginalized individuals. Many of those accused were vulnerable members of society, often elderly women living on the fringes of their communities.

In the centuries that followed, the memory of the Lancashire witches faded into history, and the county underwent significant changes. Today, Lancashire is known for its vibrant culture, stunning landscapes, and rich heritage. Yet, the legacy of the witch trials endures as a stark reminder of the dark forces of fear and superstition that once gripped this corner of England.

Chapter 38: The Staffordshire Mole Man

Beneath the picturesque landscapes of Staffordshire, England, lies a subterranean world of caves, tunnels, and passageways that have captivated the imagination of locals for generations. Within this labyrinthine realm dwells an enigmatic and elusive figure known as the "Staffordshire Mole Man." This mysterious being, whose existence remains shrouded in myth and speculation, adds an intriguing layer to the region's folklore.

Staffordshire, with its rich history and geological diversity, has long been a hub of exploration for enthusiasts of underground landscapes. Caves and tunnels, some dating back centuries, crisscross beneath the surface, revealing a hidden world of natural wonder and historical significance.

The legend of the Staffordshire Mole Man centres on a solitary figure said to inhabit these subterranean depths. Descriptions of the Mole Man vary, but common elements include tales of a reclusive recluse who wears tattered clothing and possesses an uncanny knowledge of the underground passages.

Stories about the Mole Man have circulated among locals for decades, with reports of sightings and encounters occurring sporadically. Some claim to have glimpsed the Mole Man while exploring caves or tunnels, while others recount eerie echoes and whispers heard deep within the earth.

The enigma of the Staffordshire Mole Man has given rise to a host of theories and speculations. Some believe that he is a hermit or adventurer who has chosen to live beneath the earth's surface, away from the prying eyes of the world above. Others suggest that he may be a guardian or protector of the underground realm, watching over the hidden treasures and secrets buried within.

For sceptics, the legend of the Mole Man may be dismissed as the product of local folklore, imaginative storytelling, and the eerie atmosphere of underground exploration. They argue that the subterranean world of Staffordshire, with its dark passageways and echoing chambers, can evoke a sense of mystery and wonder that gives rise to tales of supernatural beings.

Nonetheless, the Staffordshire Mole Man continues to be a subject of fascination and intrigue for those who explore the region's underground landscapes. Whether seen as a guardian of the subterranean world or a product of collective imagination, the legend of the Mole Man adds an element of mystery to the geological wonders of Staffordshire.

Chapter 39: The Yorkshire Wolds Phantom

Amidst the rolling hills and ancient landscapes of the Yorkshire Wolds, a region steeped in history and mystery, there exists a tale that has intrigued locals and visitors alike—the legend of the Yorkshire Wolds Phantom. This spectral figure, said to wander the lonely paths and quiet byways of the wolds, is a story that brings chills and wonder to those who dare to explore this remote and enigmatic part of England.

The Yorkshire Wolds, characterized by its undulating hills, picturesque villages, and quiet beauty, have long been a source of inspiration for artists and writers. Yet, beneath the serene exterior of the wolds lies a history rich in folklore and tales of the supernatural.

The Yorkshire Wolds Phantom is described as a shadowy and elusive figure, often seen on moonlit nights when the countryside is bathed in ethereal light. Witnesses report a tall, cloaked figure that appears to glide silently along the ancient pathways, leaving no trace of its passing.

Legends surrounding the Yorkshire Wolds Phantom are varied and sometimes contradictory. Some view the apparition as a guardian spirit, watching over the land and its people, while others see it as an omen of misfortune or tragedy, foretelling events yet to come.

Encounters with the Yorkshire Wolds Phantom are often described as eerie and unsettling, with witnesses left with an uncanny sense of being watched or accompanied by a presence they cannot fully explain. The figure's origins remain a mystery, with some believing it to be the spirit of a long-departed traveller or a guardian of ancient secrets.

Sceptics and believers alike have sought to unravel the enigma of the Yorkshire Wolds Phantom. Some argue that the sightings can be attributed to natural phenomena, such as the play of shadows and moonlight on the landscape, while others maintain that the figure is a genuine and otherworldly presence.

Regardless of its true nature, the Yorkshire Wolds Phantom continues to be a source of fascination and intrigue in this remote and hauntingly beautiful region of England. It serves as a reminder that, in the quiet corners of the world, mysteries and legends can endure, waiting to be discovered by those who seek to explore the shadows on the wold.

Chapter 40: The Lambton Worm

In the verdant landscapes of County Durham, nestled along the banks of the River Wear, there exists a legendary tale that has captivated the hearts and minds of generations—the story of the Lambton Worm. This formidable creature, part serpent and part dragon, represents a unique fusion of folklore and history, where a curse, a hero, and a terrifying beast converge.

The Lambton Worm legend is said to date back to the early medieval period, and its origins are interwoven with the history of the Lambton family, who resided in Lambton Castle near the village of Washington. The story begins with a young heir named John Lambton, whose ill-fated decision to go fishing one Sunday would set in motion a chain of events that would haunt his family for generations.

As the young John Lambton cast his fishing line into the River Wear, he never could have anticipated the strange and grotesque creature that he would unwittingly draw from the depths of the water. The beast that emerged was a sight to behold—an enormous and writhing worm, its body coiled and covered in slime, with eyes that glowed with malevolence.

Faced with the hideous creature before him, John Lambton made a hasty and fateful decision. He determined that the only way to rid himself of the worm was to toss it down a nearby well and be done with it. Little did he know that this act would unleash a curse that would haunt his family and his village for generations to come.

The Lambton Worm, far from being vanquished, grew in size and malevolence, terrorizing the countryside and feasting on livestock and villagers alike. Its fiery breath and insatiable appetite struck fear into the hearts of all who encountered it, and it seemed that no one could stop its rampage.

The Lambton family, plagued by the curse, sought guidance from local wise men and scholars. They learned that the only way to rid themselves of the worm's curse was to defeat the creature and then have the victor's armor cleansed in a nearby stream. However, facing such a formidable foe was no easy task.

In a dramatic showdown, John Lambton, now a knight, returned to confront the beast he had unwittingly unleashed. Armed with an assortment of weapons and protected by a suit of armor that deliberately left out one piece—the helmet—John faced the Lambton Worm in a fierce battle.

After a gruelling and perilous fight, John Lambton emerged victorious, slicing the worm into countless pieces. However, in his haste, he had failed to heed the curse's warning and neglected to cleanse himself of its taint by dipping into the stream as instructed.

The Lambton Worm had been defeated, but the curse endured, afflicting the Lambton family for generations to come. The story of the Lambton Worm became a cautionary tale of the consequences of rash decisions and the enduring power of curses.

Today, the legend of the Lambton Worm lives on in County Durham's folklore and traditions. The story serves as a reminder that choices have consequences, and curses, once unleashed, can haunt a family for centuries.

Whether seen as a cautionary fable or a testament to the enduring power of folklore, the Lambton Worm continues to be a cherished part of County Durham's rich cultural heritage.

Epilogue

As we close this book, it's my hope that these tales have stirred your curiosity and sparked your imagination. These stories remind us that there are still corners of our world that defy explanation and challenge our understanding. They invite us to question, to explore, and to marvel at the mysteries that surround us.

Whether you're a believer in cryptids or a sceptic, I hope this book has offered you a glimpse into a world that dwells just beyond our everyday reality. A world where the Loch Ness Monster might just be lurking beneath the waves, where The Welsh Dragon soars through our dreams, and where The Northumberland Hairy Haggis roams unseen.

In this journey through cryptids, monsters, myths and legends of the UK, we've seen that truth can indeed be stranger than fiction. And while we may not have all the answers, we're left with a sense of wonder and a thirst for more.

So, keep exploring. Keep questioning. And remember - there's always another mystery waiting just around the corner.

Printed in Great Britain
by Amazon

42119521R10050